THOUGHTS OF

THE 13th STEP SUCCESS MANIFESTO

As above, so below

Table of Contents

Foreword

Introduction

Step 1:
What do you want?
Step 2:
Self-esteem
Step 3:
Self-talk
Step 4:
Knowledge is Power
Step 5:
Concentration Improvement
Step 6:
Self Organizing
Step 7:
Taking Charge
Step 8:
Application
Step 9:
Group Activity
Step 10:
Life Force
Step 11:
The Power House
Step 12:
The Brain
Step 13:
Mental Attitude

Conclusion and action to take.

Dedication
This book was inspired by Napoleon Hill book, Think and Grow Rich by Tom Butler-Bowdon, published on 23/04/2009

Foreword

Being successful in life and achieving your goals is something that you can easily do. All it takes is mastering certain basic techniques and routines. The following book will provide you with 13 proven steps on how to use logical thinking to live a free and happy life. Career success and wealth only happen once you have consciously committed and planned accordingly.

THE 13th STEP SUCCESS MANIFESTO
How to become the person you inspire to be and Live Free.

Introduction

The purpose of this manual is to make you become more aware of your responsibility in your environment, and why certain things are the way they are, and their purpose in your daily activities.

You are now being initiated to a philosophy that will change your way of thinking, and give you full power over your life choices.

This manual will increase your understanding of human nature (species), and how you can make yourself more effective in your immediate environment.

In this manual, you will discover simple techniques and exercises, using logical thinking to plan, set and achieve your goals (dreams).

This manual will answer some of your dearest and deepest questions about life, questions such as why some people succeed in life and others fail.

Before you begin applying the 13 steps outlined in this manual, it is necessary to first prepare your mind to receive it.

The following exercise will aid in preparing your mind to digest the content you will be learning in this manual.

- Week 1: Unplug from your reality: - Stop listening to music, watching News and social media.
- Week 2: Changing your music genre.
- Week 3: Start watching films and TV programs that reflect success to you.

It's important you keep to this routine, due to the beneficial psychological effect it has over your mind. You will soon come to understand that your mind works best with routines, and by breaking your usual routines, you are allowing your mind to experience new realities.

The 13 steps outlined in this manual will guide you through a complete application of self-discipline techniques, to make you take control of your life, and become the master of your destiny.

STEP 1:
What do you want?

The first step for living a successful life is knowing and identifying your desires.

The problem most people face in life is identifying what their life purpose is. The problem with this way of thinking is limiting thinking, because you are unconsciously conditioning your mind to believe that life is a destination, when in reality, life is not a destination; life is a journey. Your true mission in life is to co-create experiment and experience life to its fullest potential.

Think of it this way; let's say life was like a supermarket, you have many options of where to shop but it's entirely up to you to decide which store you wish to shop from. Of course, your financial status might affect your choice of where to shop, and this is no different with your life choices; your self-beliefs will determine which experience you get to experience in your life.

HOW TO SET A GOAL

The first step in achieving success in life is your ability to set and stay focused, but before you can set a realistic and achievable goal, you need to know the difference between ambitions and goals. Ambitions are motivating feelings that make people feel they are part of a group or society, while a goal is a detailed action plan that will fulfil that feeling of you belonging in a group or society.

Now, let's set some goals; you will need a fresh notebook and a working pen. You will keep this notebook dear to you, as it will hold important information about your future. In the notebook, on a fresh page, you will write in capital letters, **'THE PERSON I INTEND TO BECOME'** and below the heading, write down all of your ambitions and all the things you want to have and achieve in life. There is no limit, there is nothing to be ashamed of; write down all of your desires, all the things you want to experiment with and experience in this life time, - write them all down. Don't worry about spelling mistakes, as long as you can go back and read it.

This notebook will be used as a drawing board for the creation of your new reality, and should be kept private. It will also be useful if you make it as a habit to carry your notebook with you everywhere you go; so whenever you feel inspired or you get an idea that will contribute to your new found reality, write it down in the notebook immediately.

STEP 2:
Self-esteem

You need faith to achieve your goals; faith is the fuel that powers you in achieving your goals because of its spiritual nature. I say spiritual because faith is invisible; faith is a state of mind which the invisible intelligent force of nature uses to communicate with you.

The method in which you develop faith where it does not already exist is EXTREMELY difficult to describe in words because you can only develop faith through emotions, feelings and affirmations.

HOW TO DEVELOP FAITH

There is one important point about our nature as human beings that I need to bring to your attention. We are an emotional, feeling, driven species experiencing a physical reality; this statement of fact is what makes faith one of the most powerful tools you can use in achieving success in your life.
Going back to your notebook list in the order of priority, which of your desires do you wish to accomplish first, second, and so forth?

Once you have completed listing your desires, the next step will be to identify where these desires stemmed from; the aim of this exercise is for you to identify the motivating feelings and emotions behind your desires. Once you have identified the motivating feelings and emotions behind your desires, then your next step will be to speak your desire into existence by affirming your motivating feeling and emotion, as already accomplished in the present tense while thinking about your desire.

Gradually, by regular practice, you will start to feel and notice your belief level in your ambition increase to the point where you will become happy, without even actually acquiring your goal.

To reach this state of mind is what people call having faith, because within yourself, you know what it is that you desire, and with great certainty, you believe it's possible for you to actually have it. This is because you feel worthy of being in possession of it, and you no longer worry about it because you know it's yours in due time.

Building faith where it does not already exist requires hard work and patience, like a gardener.
Before a gardener plants a tree, he/she first decides which tree he wishes to grow; he/she then selects the right environment and condition to plant. Gardeners are fully aware that they need to assist their plantation on its natural growth process by watering the plant, getting rid of the weeds, etc. until the plant grows to a mature tree.

It takes 10 years to grow an Oak tree; depending on which tree you desire to grow, you must prepare yourself to put in the work, and have the patience required to accomplish your goal. Just like the gardener, you need to select the right environment and condition to develop the proper belief level required to achieve your goal.

The environment and the people you surround yourself with has a lot to do with the way you think, dress, speak, and even your eating habits are partially influenced by your surroundings and environment. This statement is eye opening if you really think about it. Just THINK for a second, you are who you are because of the thoughts and vibrations you pick up through the stimuli of your daily environment.

One important thing you need to know is that negative influences and environments weaken you mentally, and makes you lose your self-confidence.

The following affirmation will act as a protecting shield against negative environments, and surroundings.

APPLICATION TECHNIQUE
FOR SELF-CONFIDENCE

I know that I have the ability to achieve the object of my definite purpose in life; therefore, I demand of myself persistence, continuous action toward its attainment, and I here and now promise to render such action - this should be recited daily throughout the day, and when opposed by negativity.

I realize the dominating thoughts of my mind will eventually reproduce themselves in outward, physical action, and gradually transform themselves into physical reality; therefore, I will concentrate my thoughts for thirty minutes daily upon the task of thinking of the person I intend to become, thereby creating in my mind a clear mental picture of that person - we will create this person in a moment; for now, let's continue.

I know, through the principle of auto-suggestion, any desire that I persistently hold in my mind will eventually seek expression through some practical means of attaining the object back of it, therefore, I will devote ten minutes daily, demanding of myself the development of self-confidence - and this will be done by reciting this daily affirmation.

I fully realize that no wealth or position can long endure, unless built upon truth and justice, therefore, I will engage in no transacting which does not benefit all whom it affects. I will succeed by attracting to myself the forces I wish to use, and the cooperation of other people.

I will induce others to serve me, because of my willingness to serve others. I will eliminate hatred, envy, jealousy, selfishness, and cynicism, by developing love for all humanity, because I know that a negative attitude towards others can never bring me success. I will cause others to believe in me, because I will believe in them, and in myself.

I will sign my name to this formula, commit it to memory, and repeat it aloud once a day, with full faith that it will gradually influence my thoughts and actions, so that I will become self-reliant and a successful person. - Napoleon Hill

"There are no limitations to the mind except those we acknowledge" - Napoleon Hill

"Both poverty and success are offspring of thoughts" - Napoleon Hill

STEP 3:
Self-talk

Self-talk is the agency of communication between your conscious mind and your subconscious mind. Your conscious mind is your everyday awareness, it's those thoughts you are thinking now, and your subconscious mind is the unconscious behaviours and actions you are doing now.

Through the proper application of the self-talk principle, you can influence your subconscious mind to translate your desire into actions, which will later convert your desire to its physical counterpart.

Positive self-talk works because of the dominating thoughts which you permit to remain in your conscious mind and it automatically reaches your subconscious mind and influences it.

Constant talk about your goals and inspiration influences your subconscious mind, and changes your actions and behaviours to match those (talks) thoughts. Your subconscious mind works involuntarily, whether you intentionally choose to influence it or not.

So why not choose to influence your own mind?

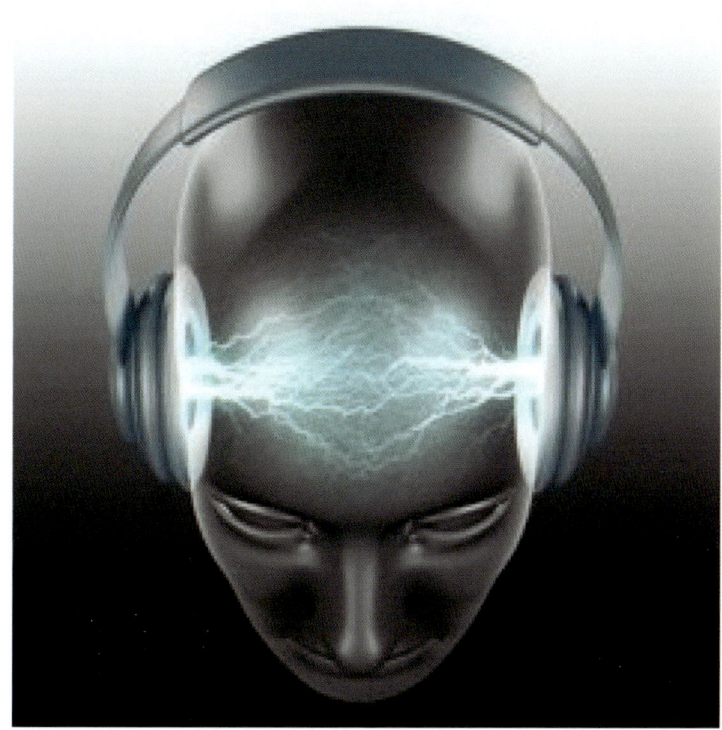

HOW TO APPLY SELF-TALK PROPERLY

The conscious mind is what protects the subconscious mind from accepting suggestions which challenge your current reality, and this is what limits most people in reaching their fullest potential in life.

You are literally unconsciously stopping yourself from reaching your fullest potential; if you want proof for this, check within yourself. Are you still doing things in your life that you consciously know are bad for you?

Your subconscious mind is influenced by your words, feelings and emotions. In order for you to properly take advantage of the self-talk principle, you have to mix your suggestions with feelings and emotions.

Going back to your notebook, - in step one, you listed your desires and aspirations; in step two, you identified your feelings and emotions behind your desires and aspirations.

Now, you are going to carry out a visualization technique that will improve your concentration, and strengthen your magnetic field to attract the necessary people and circumstances you need to live your dream life.

Concentration is key because you need to allow the images, feelings and emotions of your desires to remain in your mind while you are speaking your aspiration into existence.

VISUALISATION TECHNIQUE
Close your eyes and take a few deep breaths to relax.
Now, make your desire appear in your mind's eye.
Try to make this experience as real as possible in your mind.
Bathe yourself in the feelings and emotions behind your desire.
Stay in this state for a couple of minutes.
You will begin to get really excited about it; begin possession of your desires.
When you get to this stage, start speaking your desires into existence.

As a rule * always speak of your desires in the present tense******
Speak it like you already have it.

The above techniques should be practiced as often as possible; you will know when you have influenced your subconscious mind because you will start to get practical ideas on what you should be doing to materialize your dream life.

STEP 4:
Knowledge is Power

There are two forms of knowledge; general knowledge and specialized knowledge.
General knowledge is the information available to the masses, and specialized knowledge is simply general knowledge organized into a step by step action plan for the achievement of a goal or a purpose.

Specialized knowledge is what I am referring to when I say knowledge is power. Without a shadow of doubt, this is the best time to be alive, because you have access to unlimited source of information at your fingertips (the internet).

Now, I am going to show you how you can start organizing yourself by taking advantage of the information that is available to anyone that has access to the internet.

In order for you to organize information effectively for the attainment of your goals, it's essential that you research your goal.

You should research and study the people who are already where you want to be; study their behaviours, their routines, read their biographies, get to know them personally and if possible, get to know what makes them tick ...

This information will be useful to you, because you will have to implement it in your life. Not all of the information you will find about these people will be useful to you, - use your feelings to help you make a judgement on which bits of the information you should apply in your life.

You should learn to trust your feelings over your logical thinking, because logical thinking is based on structures and orders instructed to you, consciously or unconsciously, by you or by your environment and the people around you e.g. Family, Friends, teachers, etc.... Logical thinking has its advantages for keeping you in check with your environment; however, by trusting your feelings over logical thinking, you are putting yourself in direct communication with the invisible intelligent force of nature trusting that the universe is perfect and has your best interest.

**Warning: a proper balance must be maintained between logical thinking and feelings. If you overthink, you will never get anything done; and if you are too much into your feelings, you'll never get anything done.

Your feelings will tell you which information or ideas you need to implement. Failure on your part for not taking action on your feelings will show in the qualities of the results you will produce in setting your intention.

Remember, there is level*, this is the same way you can have two people selling the exact same product, but one person is still getting more customers than the other. This is all due to the level of commitment the person who has more customers has in trusting and taking action based on their feelings.

STEP 5:
Concentration Improvement

In this step, I am going to show you practical exercise to further enhance your concentration ability to attract to yourself the life of your dreams, using your imagination.

Imagination is the workshop of our mind. As mentioned by all of the greatest teachers of the past, "If you can imagine it, you can achieve it."

There are two forms of imagination that I will discuss here; Synthetic Imagination and Creative Imagination.

Synthetic Imagination; It's logic thinking; it is everything that you have physically seen, touched, heard, smell and tasted.

Creative Imagination; It's your link with everything and everyone, seen and unseen, that exists in the Universe. This form of imagination is where all of the greatest teachers, leaders, inventors or anyone with an astonishing achievement goes to get the "genius" ideas.

You have probably used this form of imagination to come up with a solution to a situation without even being consciously aware of using it; the greatest thing about this (our imagination) faculty is that it works automatically, without you being aware of its working.

Neither of these forms of imagination is good or bad with the proper use.
I will focus on Creative Imagination because the majority of people don't really use it, and if they do, it is usually by mere chance.

HOW TO USE CREATIVE IMAGINATION

You can dramatically improve every aspect of your life using creative imagination.

The creative imagination only works when your conscious mind is caused to vibrate at an exceedingly rapid rate by an emotion.

In the following exercise, I will show you a simple practical way to cause your mind to vibrate at a rapid rate.

It's best to carry out this exercise with your eyes closed; so make sure you are in a safe environment where you won't be disturbed or injured, as this exercise requires you to keep your eyes closed.

You will proceed in this way;
Close your eyes and get yourself comfortable
Take some deep slow breaths
Breathe in to the count of five, and then breathe out for a count of five
Slowly allowing yourself to just be here and now, present with your thoughts
Let your thoughts flow normally; just observe them as they flow in your mind
Now, start thinking about that particular goal you are working on
See it in your mind eyes as already accomplished; hold this vision in your mind.
**The trick here is for you to get really emotional about this goal
Start to intensify your emotions until your mind is filled with excitement of you achieving this desired goal.

How will you know if you are doing the exercise correctly? Your mind will get so excited that you will wake back to your normal waking state.

When this happens, stop the exercise and stay passive for few more moments.

Sometimes, what happens is that you will receive ideas, hunches and inspiration, and practical action steps of what to do to achieve your goal straight away; and on some occasion, it takes hours but no more than seven days. If this happens, open your eyes and write the ideas down on your notebook immediately.

Don't be discouraged if you don't get anything on your first attempt or straight away; the idea is for you to set your intention to your subconscious mind, and let it go.

Ideas will come to you in unlimited ways; just be observant of your thoughts and surroundings after you have carried out the concentration exercise.

***It's recommended that when carrying out the concentration exercise, you speak your goals out loud or preferably, mentally your goal; for example, if your goal is a new job, you will say out loud; NEW JOB, NEW JOB, NEW JOB, if your goal is a car, you will say NEW CAR, NEW CAR, NEW CAR…..

STEP 6:
Self Organizing

To know how to organize yourself helps you to create practical plans and action steps for you goal; however, this process is one of the most challenging steps in transforming your desire into its material counterpart, because it tests your willpower and your ability to stick to your talk and plans. No wonder many people meet failure here.

Now, I will share several formulas with you that I discovered and really impacted me in a positive way. When I had nothing, these formulas transformed me from being completely broke with no qualifications to assistant construction operation manager in 24 months.

I can't overstress the importance of this step; this is the 20% work you do to get the 80% result. This step prepares you for the fight people face when creating their own reality and destiny.

It will be very beneficial for you to create or to affiliate yourself with a mastermind alliance; this is beneficial to you because it expands your natural ability to communicate to a higher mind than yourself, therefore, allowing you to make quicker and clearer decisions and plans for the attainment of your dream life.

What you think about, talk about, associate yourself with, you become. This fact is a priceless gift that I will explain in more depth in the Mastermind Alliance Step. For now, I will proceed with an explanation of failure.

Failure is the enemy of Success, and because you aspire to become successful, this means failure is also your enemy; an enemy which you must learn to eliminate and defeat if encountered, because when failure strikes you, it strikes to kill your dreams and it's very persistent.

Failure is not good; you hear people sometimes say, 'you need to fail in order to get back up and show courage.' This statement is not so true; failure is not good sometimes and never.

Don't get me wrong here, a time will come when you will have to face this nasty bug you call failure, and when that time arrives, worry not! You will be well prepared to fight this nasty bug persistently to the point at which you'll become bigger than this enemy (failure), and have it under your submission with the tools I am now going to show you.

Think of failure as a nasty cold; you know that cold that nags you, giving you a blocked nose, headaches, burning eyes etc...

I really want you to use your imagination on this exercise; you know that worse cold you don't want to get ever again? Think of this cold as failure.

Just bear with me, it will all start making sense to you. Let me ask you a question, what do you do when you get sick?

That's right; you can either visit a doctor, or go to a pharmacist right? Okay, looking back to our illustration of failure being like a cold, when faced with failure, instead of going to visit a doctor or a pharmacist, you should consult your mastermind alliance for a cure.

When seeking for a cure from your mastermind alliance, you should be direct with them, this is why it is so important to have a mastermind alliance; but if you are not yet part of a mastermind alliance, proceed in this way;

Conceal your intentions without directly relating the failure to you, using language such as, "I watched a film" "a friend of mine," Ask people their opinions and point of views on the subject; this way, you are removing yourself from the story, allowing others to be open and honest with you, as they will be under the impression you are talking about someone else. This way, they will be more open to giving their view on the subject without worrying about hurting your feelings, or challenging your views. Listen very carefully to their advice, and remember to go with your feelings; if what they are telling you makes you feel good and brings back hope to your dreams, implement your new ideas into action and plan at once.

Now, you have a better understanding of how to deal with failure. Let's move on to the practical application of self organizing.

PRACTICAL APPLICATION OF SELF ORGANIZING

No matter what your calling is, my intention of writing this manual is to make you become more self-aware, because becoming more conscious of self will increase your possibility of living a more happy and fulfilled life.

The following exercise is going to help you have a deeper understanding on what it means by personal service.

Now, using your imagination, I would like you to let your creative mind come alive with me; what I would like you to do now is to imagine yourself connecting with me now, feel yourself merging with me, imagine in your mind's eye that you are seeing yourself through my body, likewise, I am doing the same with you now.

The purpose for this exercise is to increase your awareness of the fact that we are all connected, and everything you do to or for others, in reality, you are actually doing it to yourself or for yourself.

Most people are unconsciously conditioned to listen to other people's opinion over their own. By daily application of the above exercise, you will increase self-trust, and your ability to listen and take your own advice.

You will notice a transformation within yourself once you truly start believing and seeing yourself in others. No matter the bad you see in others, you will no longer try to force them to change or criticize them; instead, you will feel acceptance for who they are, more likely, you will try to improve those imperfections within yourself.

Likewise, every good you will see in others, you will incorporate that into yourself because you are one with all and everything.

When and how to apply
For work

Now, I am going to show you how to apply for work by means of advertising your personal service; the exercise I am going to show you here can be applied to anything you desire.

The following steps are simply listed here for the purpose of providing you with real life practical applicable skills; you can start applying immediately to improve your life.

I am going to be focusing on employment to give a fair advantage to everyone. I am fully aware that not everyone has the financial means or help to materialize their materialistic goals; for this reason, I will show you how to apply for any work/ job you desire.

I strongly believe that, in order to live happily, you must first secure your necessities like food, clothes and shelter. Once you have secured these necessities, you will then be in a better place to begin your work of becoming the master of your life and destiny.

This particular exercise is designed to help anyone without any financial means to get back on their feet, and the first step to getting back on your feet is to prepare a professional CV and cover letter.

It's very important to personalize your CV and cover letter to the employer you desire to work for, because a personalized CV and cover letter shows the employer your willingness to work for them and the effort you went through in applying for the role.

The average person uses the same CV and cover letter to apply for every job; but you don't have to be average. Personalizing your CV and cover letter to the employer you desire to work for makes you stand out from the other 1000 applicants.

The second step is applying for roles that will support your immediate needs, e.g. food and shelter. These necessities are essential, especially if your desire is to own your own business. Your mind will work more powerfully for you when you focus it on one goal at a time. If you are still worrying about where your next meal is going to come, I strongly suggest you should focus on securing this necessity first.

Now, I am going to show you how to create a professional CV and cover letter, which will make you more likely to be invited for an interview.

Your CV should be laid out in this way:

- **Your full name as the heading, centered, and bold**
- Right underneath your name, insert your email address and contact number
- Now create a new line
- **Write Key skills in capital and bold, left align it as a subheading**
- Right underneath Key skills, bullet point list all of your relevant skills
- **Write Academic achievements in capital and bold, left align it as a subheading**
- Right underneath Academic achievements, bullet point list all of your academic achievements including the institution name and location
- **Write Work experience in capital and bold, left align it as a subheading**
- Right underneath Work experience, list all of your relevant work experience including company name, location, start date and termination date.
- **Write hobbies and interests in capital and bold, left align it as a subheading**
- Right underneath hobbies and interests, bullet point list all other skills and achievements you have and are doing. Also, take this as an opportunity to list your business if you have one or planning to have, however, mention it as your hobby, not as work.
- **Write Reference in capital and bold, left align it as a subheading**
- Right underneath reference, write available on request

Your Cover letter should be laid out in this way:
Brief of experience
Jayden M. Williams
Applying for the position of
Assistant to the Project Manager of
The Success Company,
London

- **Write Reference in capital and bold education,** List relevant qualifications you have that will be of benefit for the position you are applying for.
- **Write Reference in capital and bold experience**, list all relevant experience you have which makes you suited for the position
- **Write Reference in capital and bold references,** get at least two written recommendation for the position you are applying for from either a former employer, a teacher under whom you studied, or people whose judgment may be relied upon.
- **Photograph of yourself,** interest a recent unmounted photograph of yourself
- **Write Reference in capital and bold apply for a (xxx) specific position,** here is where you explain your understanding of the position you are applying
- **Write Reference in capital and bold qualification for the (xxx) position,** here is where you explain why you will be best suited for the position based on the job description.
- Offer to go work on probation; here is where you tell the employer your availability to start work immediately, even as a trial.

How to get the exact position you desire

There are seven basics step in getting the exact position you desire, which are as follows;

1. Decide exactly what kind of job you want. If the job doesn't already exist, perhaps you can create it.
2. Choose the company or the individual who you want to work with.
3. Study your prospective employer and chances of advancement.
4. Figure out which of your skills and abilities you can offer, plan ways and means you can provide advantageous services.
5. Forget about the usual routine of "have you got a job for me?" Whether or not there is a job opening, concentrate your energy on what you can offer.
6. Once you have a plan in mind, write a tailored professional CV and Cover letter
7. Present your CV and Cover letter to the proper person with authority, and they will do the rest.

How to keep a job

There is a philanthropist formula, which I strongly encourage you to make a habit. Habits are easily created by means of repeated suggestions to the Subconscious Mind, which I will go into in great depth in the Subconscious Mind Steps; however, the QQS formula {Quality, Quantity, Spirit} is one of the most powerful formulae out there in achieving success in all you do. The QQS, according to 'Andrew Carnegie', if applied in every activity you take, you will be setting a clear mark between yourself and the average person.

Now, I am going to share with you practical examples of how you can implement the QQS formula in your life.

Q=Quality – When you first start a task or a job, make the first day a learning day, bring with you a notebook, preferably a different one from your goal journal. This notebook will be used to record detailed description of the following;
1. The tasks that your job demands of you; obviously, the more informed you are, the better.
2. Don't be afraid to ask questions, especially the questions you think are not important to ask, and write the answers to the questions in your notebook.
3. Write down thoughts and feelings you get when you meet and get introduced to your new colleagues. It is important to write this down because if you're going to be working with them, you need to get to know them by writing down their names so you don't forget them, and write down everything that catches your attention about them or the environment.

Q= Quantity – After fully understanding what task you need to carry out, depending on the nature of your task. For simplicity's sake here, I am going to focus on employment, as you're going to be an employee of someone or a company.

1. Go back to your notes and start to create routines and tactics on your thoughts, on how you will be delivering your services.
2. Don't over think this exercise when creating your plans on how you will be delivering your services, because at this initial stage your employer's only expectation of you will be for your performance to meet the standard set on the job description; - you must deliver this without fail if you want to keep the job, or have any chance of advancement within the firm.
3. Once you have passed your probation, and have now become more competent in your new environment, you should increase the quantity of your service by adding suggestions and improving anything within the organization that you've seen that will be of benefit to the organization.

S= Spirit – This is the backbone of this formula; your spirit should be one of harmony and cooperation. Why is your spirit the backbone of this formula?

As explained, you should dedicate your first day for note taking and question asking, and you should do a lot of it, WHY? Because in order for you to give the best quality and quantity of service, you first need to harmonize your spirit with the quality of service your employer expects you to deliver.

Your spirit is the backbone of this formula because of the intention you hold in your mind while carrying out any activity. It brings more of the similar circumstances to keep reoccurring; so the notes you have been taking on your first day will be used as a script to instill the right spirit you want to convey for this job.

You should rewrite your notes like a movie script. This is how you structure your script;

- You should write your movie script as if you were watching a movie of yourself going to work.
- Your movie script should be detailed, - make it close to reality as possible; this is why you've been taking notes of everything including the feelings you were getting when introduced to your new colleagues.
- The idea here is for you to write your entire day to day activity at work in your movie script, make it one of your best days that you've ever had at work. Also, write how you want to be perceived and treated by your new colleagues. Once you are satisfied with the script you have written, you will proceed by carrying out the following exercise.

Work Script

In the morning, whilst you are still in your bed, visualize your movie script playing in your mind,
I want you to see it clearly in your mind's eye, as if you were physically there, even if you are not a visual person
I want you to describe this script in your mind; just like you would have if you were telling someone the story of how your day was at work.

This is how you affect and keep a job. Regular repetition of your script will increase your script's effectiveness.

To make your script even more powerful, start playing the script in your mind when you are at work, and when interacting with your colleagues.

Remember Power is Invisible.

When carrying out this exercise, you must really detach yourself from your reality, and attach yourself to the reality of your script, even if your current reality doesn't match your script.

Keep replaying your script in your mind; the reality of things is that people will feel the energy of your script through the vibes you will be giving off and eventually you will subconsciously reorganize yourself to make your script a reality.

In this step of self organizing, I showed you practical exercises to advertise your personal service to get the exact position you desire and keep it.

I want to take this opportunity to share with you, 'Dir. Hill's' self-inventory questions and I recommend you to ask yourself these questions each year just before setting your new year's resolution. This inventory will also help you to track your personal improvement and development.

Inventory of the self

1. Have I attained the goal which I established as my objective for this year? (You should work with a definite yearly objective to be attained as a part of your major life objective)
2. Have I delivered service of the best possible quality of which I was capable, or could I have improved any part of this service?
3. Have I delivered services in the greatest possible quantity of which I was capable?
4. Has the spirit of my conduct been harmonious and cooperative at all time?

5. Have I permitted the habit of procrastination to decrease my efficiency, and if so, to what extent?
6. Have I improved my personality, and if so, in what ways?
7. Have I been persistent in following my plans through to completion?
8. Have I reached decisions promptly and definitely on all occasions?
9. Have I permitted any one or more of the six basic fears to decrease my efficiency?
10. Have I been either over-cautious or under-cautious?
11. Has my relationship with my associates at work been pleasant or unpleasant? If it has been unpleasant, has the fault been partly or wholly mine?
12. Have I dissipated any of my energy through lack of concentration of effort?
13. Have I been open-minded and tolerant in connection with all subjects?
14. In what ways have I improved my ability to render service?
15. Have I been intemperate in any of my habits?
16. Have I expressed, either openly or secretly, any form of egotism?
17. Has my conduct toward my associates been such that it has induced them to respect me?
18. Have my opinions and decisions been based upon guesswork, or accuracy of analysis and thought?
19. Have I followed the habit of budgeting my time, my expenses and my income, and have I been conservative in these budgets?
20. How much time have I devoted to unprofitable effort which I might have used to a better advantage?
21. How may I re-budget my time and change my habits so I will be more efficient during the coming year?
22. Have I been guilty of any conduct which was not approved by my conscience?
23. In what ways have I provided more service and better service than I was paid for?
24. Have I been unfair to anyone and if so, in what way?
25. If I had been the purchaser of my services, would I be satisfied with my purchase?
26. Am I in the right vocation, and if not, why not?
27. Has the purchaser of my service been satisfied with the service I have provided, and if not, why not?
28. What is my present rating on the fundamental principle of success? (Make this rating fairly and frankly; have it checked by someone who is courageous enough to do it accurately).

As you can see, success greatly depends on your willingness to become successful through labor, ingenuity and self organizing.

Successful people are individuals who have imagination, faith, enthusiasm, persistence and who take action.

I recall in my earlier days, I used to constantly blame the government and other people for being selfish, and only caring about their own self-interest. You too will come to the realization that it's perfectly fine to focus on yourself interest first, before you start thinking about bettering your family, community and the world.

STEP 7:
Taking Charge

The Majority of people fail to achieve their goals due to procrastination and lack of taking charge. Successful people have the ability to decide promptly, and change the mind slowly after coming to a decision; the decision you make will determine the success you will experience in your life.

Procrastination is the opposite of decision, and it's an enemy that everyone must conquer.

**Special attention should be taken, as you begin to awaken your awareness to the reality of life being predominantly influenced by your thoughts (focused thoughts).

In order for you to translate a thought to its material counterpart, you must feed it your energy by concentrating the feelings you associate with that particular desire until it's materialized; and this process could take time, depending on your level of concentration and determination.

So when you decide for sure exactly what you want, you must also be willing to give this desire all the attention and action it requires. In other words, if you are the type that doesn't like seeing your ideas through, you will never achieve anything astonishing in your life. This is why it's very important to be able to make a decision and see it through; persistence and decision making are the keys that open the door to the life of your dreams.

Practical Application 1:
The technique I am now going to show you will help you to make quicker and more accurate decisions in your everyday life. It is advised that at the beginning stage, you practice this exercise with small decisions, such as which venue you should visit with your friends or where should you go for your next family vacation until you are more confident with yourself.

When faced with the opportunity to make a decision on something, you should proceed in the following way;
- Always go with the first thought that comes in your mind; at this stage, it shouldn't really matter to you if your decision is accurate or not. The idea here is for you to be persistent with your decision, and don't change your mind when others tries to convince you to follow their point of view.
- Stick to your decision no matter what! Even if others opinions start to make sense to you, don't change your mind towards their view. Stick to your decision and see it through. If it turned out to be the wrong decision, pay the price for your mistake and try again.

This exercise will also improve your ability to value your ideas and beliefs.

**Remember, if you sincerely need facts or information from people to enable you reach a decision, secure this information from them secretly without disclosing your intention to them.

Practical Application 2:
Another great habit you should develop is the habit of being secretive and keeping quiet about your true intentions.

The exercise I am going to show you will help you create the habit of being secretive, and keeping quiet about yourself. The example I am going to use in this exercise is purely to give you a base to work from, but feel free to recreate it to fit your lifestyle. I am going to use an example of someone that works from 0900-1700 five days per week. This is how you should incorporate this exercise in your routine.
- Start off first by setting an alarm clock for 12noon, and label it as quiet time, and set a second alarm 45 min later, and label this second alarm as 'how was it?'

So what do you do during these quiet times?
- You should focus your intention on yourself and anything that needs to be done at that particular time; but the trick is for you to avoid, at all costs, communicating or having conversations related to your intention or desire. You should only speak about things that are not directly related to your intention or desire to others; proceed in this way until you begin to feel comfortable with this practice, and gradually increase the length of your quiet time.

The aim of this exercise is to stop you from speaking your intention to others without first putting it into action.

Power in Nature

One important thing you should be made aware of is that every time you open your mouth in the presence of a person who has an abundance of knowledge, you display to that person your exact stock of knowledge or your lack of it. Also, every person with whom you associate is, like yourself, seeking the opportunity to improve themselves, and if you talk about your plans too freely, you may be surprised when you learn that some other person has beaten you to your goal by putting them into action ahead of you. The plans of which you talked unwisely, genuine wisdom is usually noticeable through modesty and silence. "Napoleon Hill - Author"

The proper understanding and faithful application of the practical exercise mentioned in this success manual will set you free to live the life of your dreams.

There are six key steps in this manual that you must take special care to follow; because these six steps are the steps you will be constantly battling with, especially if you are not yet living the life of your dreams.

I strongly believe these six steps are what make the difference between the life you want to live, and the struggle people face in not living a fulfilled life.

1. Want: you must have a desire for something (you must want something)
2. Taking charge: You must decide on what you want to achieve
3. Self-talk: You must believe that your desire is achievable
4. Application: You must see your idea through
5. Group activity: You must be willing to seek help from other people with similar motives to your own.
6. Organized Planning: You must organize yourself by creating action plans that will lead to the attainment of your goals.

You are guaranteed to materialize any of your dreams, by just mastering the above mentioned six steps**

STEP 8
Application

Actual application of your action steps is essential for achieving a goal, and also for the development of persistence.

The method in which you activate persistence is by the application of your action steps through the aid of your will-power.

Will power is your ability to make yourself to do what you set yourself to do, however, if you have a weak desire for something you might find it difficult to stick with your plans.

You effortlessly activate your will-power by having a big desire, so much so that when you think about the lack of the desired objective it makes you feel useless in life or even worse, almost suicidal. If you want something this bad, I can guarantee you are half way to achieving it.

It's very important you understand that before you can accomplish any goal, you should first bring about that consciousness in yourself. Only then you will be able to attract to yourself your desired goal.

You should keep in mind, at all times, that the starting point of all achievement is the desire for it. A weak desire brings a weak result; you should have faith in your plans, knowing that the invisible force of nature is moving circumstances for you, and be patient and wait for the perfect time.

I strongly encourage you to commit to, and persistently apply all the exercises I have shown you in this manual until they become your fixed habits (second nature).

It usually takes up to 90 days to create a habit, depending on the beliefs that you already hold.

Without you acquiring persistence, you will be defeated before you even begin. 'Poverty is attracted to the one whose mind is favorable to it, as success is attracted to him whose mind has been deliberately prepared to attract it.'

There are no other ways you can develop the necessary consciousness you need to achieve your desires if you're not persistently taking actions towards your goals. I personally believe that there is a hidden Guide whose duty is to test us with all sorts of discouraging experiences. **This hidden Guide lets no one enjoy great achievement without first passing the test of persistence, and** those who can't take it simply don't make the grade, Those who can take it are bountifully rewarded for their persistence; and as compensation they receive their pursued desire and knowledge every failure bring (which is equivalent to advantage).

Persistence is a state of mind which can be developed like any other state of mind. Persistence is truly what separates the men from the boys. There are eight habits that lead to the development of persistence which are as follows;

- **Definiteness of purpose -:** You should decide on what you really want
- **Desire -:** You should have an intense desire to get what you want
- **Self-reliance -:** You should accept your current situation for what it is, and believe in your ability to transform it to whatever you desire it to be.
- **Definiteness of plans -:** You should organize yourself by creating definite action steps towards the attainment of your goals. It doesn't matter if you think your plan is going to work or not; the trick is to just start somewhere, and keep improving as you see fit. Remember, any positive action toward your goal is better than no action.
- **Accurate knowledge -:** Avoid guess work when creating action steps for your goals; your information should be based on experiences or on observation of the people whom are already in possession of what you want; and if that thing you desire has never been created, observe nature and listen to your feelings.
- **Co-operation -:** You should sympathize, understand and harmonize yourself with like-minded people. It also tends to help in the development of persistence.
- **Will-power -:** You should think about your dreams all the time, while focusing your intention to constant improvement of your action steps along the way until you materialize your desire.
- **Habit -:** Persistence is the direct result of habits. The mind absorbs and becomes part of its daily environment and experiences; whatever you feed your mind daily, becomes your second nature and creates a new habit.

Persistence is essential for success and living a fulfilled life. The following list will help you to identify with yourself if you lack persistence. If you identify that you lack persistence, you can overcome this weakness by the practical exercises I have been showing in this manual.

SYMPTOMS OF LACK OF PERSISTENCE

- **Failure to recognize and to clearly define exactly what you want -:** What do you want? A house or money?
- **Procrastination, with or without cause. (usually backed up with alibis and excuses) -:** I am tired; I will do it tomorrow.
- **Lack of interest in self-organizing -:** Take a course or become an apprentice
- **Indecision, the habit of blaming others for your own mistakes instead of facing issues squarely (also backed with alibis) -:** Once you make a decision, avoiding taking responsibility for your actions.
- **The habit of relying upon alibis, instead of creating definite plans for the solution to your problems -:** You have decided to save 300 pounds every month, and a friend comes to tell you about a party. Don't spend your money**
- **Self-satisfaction -:** You should never entertain the idea that you are satisfied if you still have desires for self-improvement.
- **Indifference, usually reflected in your readiness to compromise on all occasions, rather than meeting opposition and fighting it -:** Fight for what you believe in.
- **The habit of blaming others for your mistakes and accepting unfavourable circumstances as being unavoidable -:** You are who you think you are. Nothing happens to you without first being created and accepted by you.
- **Weakness of desire, due to neglect in the choice of motives that impel action -:** The sky is the limit; if you aim for the moon, even if you miss it, you will land in the stars, still above earth :)
- **Willingness, even eagerness to quit at the first sign of defeat. (based upon one or more of the six basic fears)**
- **Lack of writing an organized plan -:** You must write all of your dreams and thoughts on paper.
- **The habit of neglecting to move on ideas, or to grasp opportunity when it presents itself -:** TAKE ACTION!!
- **Wishing instead of willing -:** Wishes don't come true, actions and goals do.
- **The habit of compromising with poverty instead of aiming at riches -:** In my organization 'Thoughts Of Success,' we support and remind individuals of their Major Goal, and help them with regular training to prepare their mind for the hardship one can face in the pursuit of a dream.
- **Searching for all the shortcuts to success, trying to get without giving a fair equivalent, usually reflected in the habit of gambling -:** Remember, there is no shortcut to success. To be successful requires hard work and dedication; it's best I tell you this now to save you from disappointment if you're thinking that the road to success is easy.
- **Fear of criticism, failure to create plans and to put them into action, because of what other people will think, do or say. This enemy belongs at the head of the**

list, because it generally exists in your subconscious mind, where its presence is not recognized (see the six basic fears in a later chapter) -; **You should become aware that people will always be judging; it doesn't matter what you do. People don't generally care about what you do, as long as you are not threatening their own selfish idea of you.**

You have now been equipped with valuable information that will help you see your ideas through.

It's crucial that you develop the habit of seeing your ideas through. To me personally, persistence is by far 'the most' valuable habit anyone could possess. This is why I have summarized it in four simple steps for you to follow, in order to increase your chances of being more persistent in the pursuit of your dream life.

1. **A definite purpose backed by a burning desire for its fulfilment:** A definite purpose could be that you want; a job that will pay £2000 a month, because without this job, you don't see yourself being able to accommodate your basic survival needs, or the lack of having a job makes you envy others.
2. **A definite plan, expressed in continuous action:** This means you should start sending a CV every day until you get that job. At the same time, you should be open minded for any other job offers that will give you money to fulfil your immediate needs, but never get lost in that job or you will forget your goal.
3. **A mind closed tightly against all negative and discouraging influences, including negative suggestions from relatives, friends and acquaintances:** You should remember that no one knows your desire more than you; so it's best not to talk about your desire unwisely to people, especially to those that have nothing positive to suggest.
4. **A friendly alliance with one or more persons who will encourage you to follow through your plans and purpose:** Go to event or places where you are likely to meet people who are already doing or have what you desire, and be friends with them, and keep them close to you.

STEP 9
Group Activity *(Mastermind Alliance)

Being part of an organized group allows you to use other people's knowledge to create a comprehensive and contemplated action plan for the attainment of your goals.

There is an invisible power that is available through a properly selected Master Mind group. As defined by Napoleon Hill, The MasterMind Alliance is a coordination of knowledge and effort, in a spirit of harmony between two or more people for the attainment of a definite purpose.

There are two advantages in being part of a MasterMind group, which are;

Advantage number one: Economic advantage; this is created by surrounding yourself with the advice, counsel and personal cooperation of a group of men or women who are willing to lend to you wholehearted aid, in a spirit of perfect harmony. This form of cooperative alliance has been, and still is, the basis of nearly every great fortune. You really need to digest this concept because it will determine your financial status.

Advantage number two: The psychic; the psychic phase of the MasterMind group is much more abstract and difficult to comprehend, because it has reference to spiritual forces. *"No two minds ever come together without thereby creating a third invisible, intangible force which may be likened to a third mind."*

To have a proper understanding of the second advantage of the MasterMind Alliance, you need to be aware of the scientific fact that in the whole universe, there are only two known elements to man which are Energy and Matter. It is well-known that matter maybe broken down into units of molecules, atoms and electrons; also, there are units of matter which may be isolated, separated and analyzed. Likewise, there are units of energy.

The human mind is a form of energy; a part of it being spiritual in nature. So, when the minds of two people are coordinated in a spirit of harmony, the spiritual units of each mind forms an affinity, which constitutes the "psychic" of the MasterMind group.

Nature uses energy as her set of building blocks, out of which she constructs every material thing in the universe, including man and every form of animal and vegetable life. This is done through a process only nature completely understands, how she translates energy into matter; however, these same building blocks nature uses are also available to humans, in the energy involved in thinking.

Man's brain maybe compared to an electric battery; it absorbs energy from the other, which permeates every atom of matter and fills the entire universe. "It is a well-known fact that a group of electric batteries will provide more energy than a single battery" and the same applies to the human brain.

This is why a carefully selected MasterMind group will intensify your brain battery to materialize your goals faster than it would have taken your efforts alone; success can only take the place of poverty through well-conceived and carefully executed PLANS.

While poverty needs no plan, because poverty is bold and ruthless, and success is shy and timid, success has to be "attracted."

ANYBODY can WISH FOR SUCCESS, AND MOST PEOPLE DO. BUT ONLY A FEW KNOW THAT A DEFINITE PLAN PLUS A BURNING DESIRE TO SUCCEED ARE THE ONLY DEPENDABLE MEANS OF ACCUMULATING WEALTH AND SUCCESS. - "Napoleon Hill - Author"

STEP 10
Life Force

Life force or sexual energy is one of the most powerful human energies. Once a person is driven by this desire, he develops keenness of imagination, courage, will-power, persistence and creative ability unknown to them at other times.

So strong and impelling is the sexual energy that humans freely run the risk of life and reputation to indulge in it. However, once harnessed, it can be redirected towards your goals and use this powerful energy as a motivating creative force in any calling or profession.

The way you transmute the life force (emotion of sex) calls for the exercise of will-power. As discussed in previous steps, the bigger your desire is, the more motivation you will possess towards acquiring it.

The desire for sexual expression is inborn and natural; you should not try to submerge or eliminate this desire, instead, you should learn how to transmute (transfer) this energy.

The emotion of sex or better, the energy of sex has the possibility of three constructive potentialities, which are: -
- The perpetuation of mankind
- The maintenance of health

- The transformation of mediocrity into genius through transmutation

Sex transmutation is simple and easy, all it means is the switching of the mind from thoughts of physical expression to thoughts of some other nature.

HOW TO TRANSMUTE YOUR SEXUAL ENERGY

A simple method you can use to transmute your sexual energy is to let your sexual desire ? build up as normal when you feel the presence of the emotion of sex, while focusing your attention to your goals and dreams without letting the energy out. This is so as to cause your mind to vibrate to a higher frequency than usual, - as discussed in previous steps, this will help facilitate connection with the infinite consciousness.

The human mind responds to stimuli which excite it and cause it to vibrate in a higher vibrational rate known as, enthusiasm, creative imagination, intense desire etc....

The stimuli to which the mind responds most freely are:-

- The desire for sexual expression
- Love
- A burning desire for fame, power, or financial gain, money
- Music
- Friendship between either those of the same sex or those of the opposite sex
- A Mastermind association based upon the harmony of two or more people who ally themselves for spiritual or material advancement
- Mutual suffering, such as that experienced by people who are persecuted
- Positive self-talk
- **Fear**
- **Narcotics and alcohol**

As you can see, the desire for sexual expression comes at the head of the list of stimuli, which most effectively "set-up" the vibration of the mind, and start the "wheels" of physical action. Eight of these stimuli are natural and constructive; two are destructive.

The emotion of sex or your sexual energy is by far the most intense and powerful of all mind stimuli; by transmuting your sexual energy, it will lift you to the status of a genius.

What is a genius? A genius is a man or woman who has discovered how to increase the vibration of his/her thoughts to the point where he/she can freely communicate with sources of knowledge not available through the ordinary rate of vibration of thoughts.

You will develop the state of genius, by raising your thoughts vibration by one of the mind stimuli listed above, or by the sixth sense of creative imagination.

Most people never use the faculty of creative imagination intentionally, and if used at all, it usually happens by mere accident, and those who use this faculty intentionally with the understanding of its functions are geniuses.

The faculty of your creative imagination is your direct link between you and the infinite intelligence.

All so-called revelations referred to in religions, and all discoveries and inventions, all take place through the faculty of creative imagination.

When ideas or concepts flush into your mind, through what is popularly called a "hunch," they come from one or more of the following sources:-
- Infinite Intelligence
- Your subconscious mind, wherein is stored every sense impression and thought impulse which ever reached the brain through any of the five senses [Comment [Val]: 'ever' or 'never']
- From the mind of some other person who has just released the thought, or picture of the idea or concept, through conscious thought
- From other people's subconscious storehouse

The above lists the source from which "inspired" ideas or "hunches" may be received.

One important thing you should remember is that the creative imagination functions best when the mind is vibrating, due to some form of mind stimulation at an exceedingly high vibrational rate through one or more of the ten mind stimulants previously mentioned.

Your creative imagination has the possible effect to lift your thoughts far above the horizon of ordinary thoughts.

Creative imagination gives freedom for action, and clears the way for the sixth sense to function, by allowing the mind to become receptive to ideas which it could not have reached under any other circumstances.

The 'sixth sense' is the faculty which marks the difference between a genius and an ordinary individual; however, you can only cultivate this faculty through regular practice and use.

Now, I am going to show you practical ways you can use your creative imagination through sexual transmutation to access your source of knowledge for the accumulation of your goals.

1. Get yourself sexually aroused to the point of no return, without losing control over your urge
2. Now, concentrate on your goal; see yourself in your mind eyes. You are already living your dreams; hold this vision of you being successful or getting that job promotion in your mind for about 3-5 minutes, in order to imprint this mental picture to your subconscious mind.
3. **R**elax and clear your mind of all thoughts associated with that desire, while releasing your urge.

Ideas will then begin to flush in your mind, sometimes immediately, depending on the development of your "sixth sense".

At other times, the results are not what you expected; don't be discouraged if you don't get result from your first attempt. You will eventually harness this faculty by regular practice.

One other benefit of transmuting your sexual energy is the increase in personal magnetism.

Personal magnetism is what draws or repels people away from you. This is because **your thought vibration is felt by others, and when you mix your thoughts with the emotion of sex, it has a powerful positive influence on the people around you.**

I respect the fact that everyone has a free will to do as they please, and I encourage you to express yourself fully, because I strongly believe that life is to be enjoyed to the fullest.

** The only caution I would like to raise is this, any excess in any stimulation can destroy vital organs of the body including the brain.

Overindulgence in sex may not only destroy reason and willpower, but it may also lead to mental and emotional ill-health

Sex alone is a mighty urge to action, but its force is often uncontrollable. When the emotion of love begins to mix itself with the emotion of sex, the result is calmness of purpose, poise, accuracy of judgment and balance; however, when you are driven by the desire to please a woman, based solely upon the emotion of sex, a man may be and usually, is capable of great achievement, but his actions may be disorganized, distorted and totally destructive.

Human emotions are states of mind; nature has provided human with a chemistry of the mind which operates in a manner similar to the chemistry of matter.

It's a well-known fact that a chemist may create a deadly poison by mixing certain elements, none of which are in themselves harmful in their right proportions. Human emotions are same.

The presence of any one or more of the destructive emotions (hate, fear, jealousy etc.) in the human mind, through the chemistry of the mind can create a deadly poison which may destroy your sense of justice and fairness.

In extreme cases, the presence of any combination of these emotions in the mind may destroy your reasoning.

The emotion of sex and jealousy when mixed, may turn a person into an insane beast; the road to genius consists of the development, control, and use of your sexual energy, love and romance.

I encourage you to allow the presence of the emotion of love, sex, service and romance as the dominating thought in your mind, and discourage the presence of all destructive emotions.

You are (human) a creature of habit, and your mind thrives upon the dominating thoughts; so feed it.

*One last key point; the secret of emotion or mind control lies in the understanding of the process of transmutation.

When a negative emotion presents itself in your mind, it can be transmuted into a positive or constructive emotion by simply changing your thoughts.

Man's greatest motivating force is his desire to please woman! It is this inherent desire of man to please woman that gives woman the power to make or break a man.

Napoleon Hill quoted, "The woman who understands man's nature, and tactfully caters to his need has no fear of competition from other woman."

Men may have indomitable will-power when dealing with other men, but can be easily managed by the woman of their choice.

STEP 11
The Power House

In this step, I will go even deeper in explaining the functions of your subconscious mind.

The topic of the subconscious mind really excites me because of the effects it can have on living the life of your dreams; this is why I refer to it as the power house.

The subconscious mind has the ability to draw upon the forces of the Infinite Intelligence, and voluntarily transmute your desire into its physical equivalent by always making use of the most practical means by which your desire may be accomplished.

You cannot control your subconscious mind entirely; but you can voluntarily imprint suggestion and images to your subconscious mind which you desire to materialize or experience.

The subconscious mind consists of a field of consciousness where every thought that reaches your conscious mind through any of your five senses gets stored and filed in your mind, regardless of its nature.

The subconscious mind responds freely to your dominating desire or thought which has been mixed with emotional feelings, such as faith, sex etc.... Your subconscious mind absorbs your environment, your thoughts and the thoughts of others around you voluntarily.

My aim of writing this manual is to show you practical ways to control your mind and your environment and to make you become more aware of your surroundings.

Being in control of your environment simply means living your life consciously and being consciously aware of the fact that your subconscious mind is functioning voluntarily, whether you make any effort to influence it or not.

The subconscious mind will not remain as an ideal! If you fail to imprint your desires on it, it will feed upon the thoughts which reach it as the result of your neglect.

I am fully aware of the fact that living consciously is not an easy task, but by associating yourself with like-minded individuals, your positive thinking will mix with the positive thinking of those people around, therefore helping each of you to shut off the flow of all negativity, and voluntarily influence each other's subconscious mind with positive impulses and desires.

Voluntarily influencing your subconscious mind is the key that grants you access to the control room of your mind, and have full control of your mind and its working.

As mentioned earlier, thoughts and impulses, which have been well mixed with emotions, are acted upon more readily by the subconscious mind than thoughts and impulses that originated in "cold reasoning." The reason for this is that the subconscious mind understands best the language of emotional feelings.

Now, I am going to show you the seven major positive emotions and the seven major negative emotions; so you may draw upon the positive emotions and avoid the negative emotions when imprinting your subconscious mind.

The seven major positive emotions;
- The emotion of Desire
- The emotion of Faith
- The emotion of Love
- The emotion of Sex
- The emotion of Enthusiasm
- The emotion of Romance
- The emotion of Hope

The seven major negative emotions;
- The emotion of Fear
- The emotion of Jealousy
- The emotion of Hatred
- The emotion of Revenge
- The emotion of Greed
- The emotion of Superstition
- The emotion of Anger

Both positive and negative emotions cannot occupy the mind at the same time; one or the other must dominate. It's your responsibility to make sure positive emotions are the dominating emotions on your mind.

I do understand it might not be easy to stay positive all the time, however, by making it a habit to consciously apply positive emotions at all times, positive thinking will eventually be the dominating state of your mind and habit.

STEP 12
The Brain

Now you have reached to the core step of this manual, or as some say, you have now reached the deep end.

Now, I am going to try to explain the working of the human brain, but not in a scientific way because I am not a biologist; however, I am going to be explaining how you can use your brain to materialize your desire. **I hope I have made myself clear here.**

The human brain, in terms of manifestation acts like a broadcasting and receiving station of your thoughts, through the medium of the ether, similar to the radio broadcasting principle.

Just to clarify what the ether is; the ether is the energy field that is around everything on the galaxy. The ether is the invisible force of nature, in simple terms; the human brain is capable of releasing and picking up vibrations of thoughts which are being released by other brains.

This happens through the creative imagination, and the creative imagination works as both the receiving and the broadcasting set of the brain.

In order for you to activate this mechanism of creative imagination, the brain needs to be vibrating at an exceedingly high rate, and this is done through one of the major positive or negative emotions that I shared with you on the previous step.

Thoughts, which have been modified by or stepped-up by any of the major emotions, vibrate at a much higher rate than an ordinary thought.

Thoughts which have been modified by any of the major emotions are thoughts which can be passed from one brain to another, through the broadcasting machinery of the human brain.

When the brain is vibrating at a rapid rate, not only does it attract the thoughts and ideas released by other brains through the medium of the ether, but it also give your thoughts that "feeling" (POWER) which is essential for your thoughts to be imprinted and acted upon by the subconscious mind.

In a way, the subconscious mind could be viewed as the sending station of the brain, and the creative imagination as the receiving station of the brain, through which the vibrations of thoughts are picked up from the ether.

The subconscious mind, and the faculty of the creative imagination, constitutes the sending and receiving set of the mental broadcasting machinery and positive self talk is the medium through which you put into operation the "broadcasting station" of the brain.

STEP 13
Mental Attitude

Your mental attitude is very important in communicating with the invisible force of nature.

We have now reached the final step of this manual; the principle I have explained in this manual can only be understood by application, not theory.

And it is only right that in the final step, I should show how you can be mastering your life. And you master your life by mastering your sixth sense faculty; YES I have said it, the sixth sense.

The sixth sense is that portion of your subconscious mind which I have been referring to as the creative imagination. I also referred to it as the receiving set, through which ideas and plans flash into the mind, and these flashes are what the majority of people refer to as "hunches" or "inspiration".

Without a practical application of the techniques outlined in this manual, it would be quite difficult for you to fully understand what I am going to attempt to explain here – you see how I used the word attempt? Because what I am going to be explaining here is beyond my own understanding.

The invisible force of nature- the name is self-explanatory; these forces are invisible and can only be understood by experience.

This topic is so profound, and many people refer to this topic as miracles, but with proper understanding of the laws of nature, you will come to understand that there is no such thing as miracles, except for properly applied natural laws.

I can't really directly explain the working of the sixth sense. I can only share with you my own experiences, and the methods I use to work with the sixth sense.

You will have to wait until you have your own experience in order for you to properly understand the workings of the sixth sense.

Proper development of the sixth sense only happens after years and years of meditation and development of the mind from within. The sixth sense is a mixture of the mental and of the spiritual (invisible force of nature).

Through the aid of the sixth sense, you can be warned of impending dangers in time to avoid them; you will be notified of opportunities in time to embrace them.

Once you have developed your sixth sense, the invisible force of nature will come to your aid, and will do your bidding for you as a guardian angel who opens to you at all times the door to the temple of wisdom and opportunities.

Whether or not you believe this statement, you will truly never know the truth until you put into practice what I have outlined in this manual.

I am going to show you a practical application technique that you can start using to develop the sixth sense.

The first step in developing the sixth sense is character building. You need to build an Avatar of yourself or an alter ego, something like Clark Kent in Superman movie.

Your character will consist of a list of people who inspire you, or the person you intend to become.

This exercise requires about 30-45 min of your time; ideally it's best to be carried out every night, just before bed.

So, what you do is, you create a list of people who inspire you, think of all the great qualities, and skills these individuals possess, then mentally call these individuals for a meeting. This is all happening in your head (you are imagining this meeting taking place), visualizing it in your mind.

These individuals will therefore, formulate your invisible Mastermind group, and need not be treated any differently from the way you would in "real life". You can have as many characters as you like; it doesn't matter if the people you choose for your invisible mastermind group are dead or still alive. Once you have selected and appointed them, you will need to start arranging regular daily meetings with your invisible team.

One important point you need to remember is these imaginary people are the reflection of your imagination. Treat them with respect; you must always be the chair (in charge) of these imaginary meetings in all circumstances.

The idea behind these imaginary meetings is for you to consult your mastermind group for practical advice on how you can shape your personality in order for you to become the person you are intending to be; these individuals are going to be very useful to you from now. So, it's advised you select them very carefully, as they will be working for you behind the scene, building you into the person you aspire to become.

HOW TO CALL UP YOUR INVISIBLE MASTERMIND

1. Close your eyes and start by taking some deep breaths steadily.
2. Now, send your attention to the soles of your feet; you should feel a slight tingly feeling. At the soles of your feet, bring this tingly feeling right up, and work your way up to the top of your head.
3. Now, just relax; make your body relax as much as you can get it to relax
4. Now, start calling your characters by their names in your mind eyes one by one, best try to visualize them appearing when you call their names.
5. Once they all appear, introduce them to each other; always remember you are in charge.
6. Once you have finished with the introductions, tell them why you called them; in this case, you want them to assist in the building of your character. So you can tell them how much you appreciate the qualities they have, and ask them to assist you in developing those qualities in your personality.
7. Once you finish your meeting, wish them farewell and arrange for another appointment with them in the future.

These characters will be your team; you can call upon them whenever you need their assistance. You can call upon them individually or as a team; it's up to you, but it's recommended that you arrange a meeting with all of them at least, once a week.

This exercise might feel odd in the beginning, but through regular practice and meetings with your invisible team, you will begin to notice the benefit of this exercise.

As you can see, the topic I am covering here is a subject which the majority of people are not familiar with; you only need to develop the sixth sense if your desire is to accumulate a vast amount of wealth.

The sixth sense is not something that you can take off and put on at will; the ability to use this great power comes slowly through the application of all the steps you have been learning in this manual.

Naturally, the knowledge of the sixth sense is not available until you are well past the age of fifty; this is because of the spiritual forces so closely associated with the sixth sense.

The sixth sense does not mature and become usable, except through years of meditation, self-examination and serious thought.

I have included these steps in this manual in order to give you a complete guide by which you could guide yourself in attaining whatever you ask of life.

The starting point of all achievement is the desire, and the finishing point is that brand of knowledge which leads to understanding- understanding of self, understanding of others, understanding of the laws of nature, recognition and understanding of happiness.

This sort of understanding comes in its fullest only through familiarity, and through regular use of the sixth sense, hence, I have included the sixth sense as part of this manual for the benefit of those who demand more than just money.

My main focus in this step was to bring you to the awareness of the sixth sense, and the understanding of the invisible forces of nature.

Before you benefit from the principles you are learning in this manual, you must first remove the six ghosts of fear that prevent people from living life to the fullest.

These six basic fears are the cause of all discouragement, - timidity, procrastination, indifference, indecision, lack of ambition, lack of self-reliance, lack of initiative, lack of self-control and enthusiasm.

As you will be analyzing the "Six Ghosts of fear," you should be reminded that these fears are nothing but ghosts that exist only in your mind.

To be successful in working with the techniques shared in this manual, you need to prepare your mind to receive the benefits. It's not difficult to prepare your mind to receive the benefit of living your life to its fullest potential; all you need to do is thoroughly study, analyze, and understand the three main enemies which you need to clear out, and those enemies are; Indecision, Doubt and Fear! Your sixth sense will never function while these three negative enemies remain in your mind.

I am now going to discuss an end which must be attained before this philosophy as a whole can be put into practical use.

Also, I am going to show you how to analyze the conditions which have reduced a huge number of people to poverty.

I am going show the truth, which must be understood by all who desire to accumulate wealth, whether measured in terms of money or a state of mind of far greater value than money.

The Six Basic Fears
There are six basic fears that we all suffered at one time or another. I listed them below in order of their most appearance according Napoleon Hill.
1. The Fear of poverty
2. The Fear of criticism
3. The Fear of ill health
4. The Fear of loss of love of someone
5. The Fear of old age
6. The Fear of death

Fears are nothing more than states of mind; your mind should be controlled and directed.

These basic fears lies at the bottom of most of your worries; all other fears are of minor importance, and they can be grouped under the above mentioned six headings.

There are no compromises between poverty and wealth. The two roads that lead to poverty and wealth travel in opposite directions; if you desire wealth, you must refuse to accept any circumstance that leads towards poverty.

The starting point of the path that leads to wealth is desire; you have been given a road map in this manual which will keep you on the road to wealth, but the responsibility to walk this path is up to you. There's no one to blame but yourself if you neglect to make a start or even worse, to stop before arriving.

Fear of poverty is the most destructive of the six basic fears, and because it is the most difficult to master, the majority of people think that they don't fear anything. This is because most people don't even realize that they are tied spiritually and physically through some form of fear, so subtle that they go through life burdened with fears that they don't even recognize.

Now, I am going to show you the symptoms of each of the six basic fears; note down any of them you recognize.

SYMPTOMS OF THE FEAR OF POVERTY

- INDIFFERENCE:- Commonly expressed through lack of ambition; willingness to tolerate poverty; acceptance of whatever compensation life may offer without protest; mental and physical laziness, lack of initiative, imagination, enthusiasm and self-control.
- INDECISION: - The habit of permitting others to do your thinking for you. Staying on the fence, instead of attacking.
- DOUBT:- Generally expressed through alibis and excuses designed to cover up, explain away, or apologize for your failures. Sometimes, expressed in the form of envy of those who are successful, or by criticizing them.
- WORRY:- Usually expressed by finding fault with others, a tendency to spend beyond your income, neglect of personal appearance, expression of disapproval, displeasure, concentration, anger, over-consumption of alcoholic drink and narcotics, nervousness, lack of balance, self-consciousness and lack of self-reliance.
- OVER-CAUTION:- The habit of looking for the negative side of every circumstance, thinking and talking of possible failure, instead of concentrating upon the means of succeeding. Knowing all the roads to disaster, but never searching for the plans to avoid failure, pessimism and bad disposition.
- PROCRASTINATION:- The habit of putting off until tomorrow that which should have been done last year. Spending enough time in creating alibis and excuses to have the job done. Willingness to compromise, rather than to put up a stiff fight. Compromising with difficulties, instead of harnessing and using them as stepping stones to advancement. Bargaining with life for a penny, instead of demanding prosperity, opulence, riches, contentment and happiness. Planning what to do if and when overtaken by failure, instead of burning all bridges, and making retreat impossible. Expecting poverty, instead of demanding wealth. Association with those who accept poverty, instead of seeking the company of those who demand and receive wealth.

SYMPTOMS OF THE FEAR OF CRITICISM

- SELF-CONSCIOUSNESS:- Generally expressed through nervousness, timidity in conversation and in meeting strangers, awkward movement of the hand and of the limbs, shifting of the eyes.
- LACK OF POISE:- Nervousness in the presence of others, poor posture of the body, poor memory, and lack of voice control.
- PERSONALITY:- Lacking in firmness of decision, personal charm, and ability to express opinions definitely. The habit of side-stepping issues instead of meeting them squarely. Agreeing with others without careful examination of their opinions.
- INFERIORITY COMPLEX:- The habit of expressing self-approval by word of mouth and by actions, as a means of covering up a feeling of inferiority. Using "big words" to impress others (often, without knowing the real meaning of the words). Imitating others in dress, speech and manners. Boasting of imaginary achievements.

- **EXTRAVAGANCE:-** The habit of trying to "keep up with the Joneses," spending beyond your income.
- **LACK OF INITIATIVE:-** Failure to embrace opportunities for self-advancement, fear to express opinions, hesitancy of manner and speech, deceit in both words and deeds, lack of confidence in your own ideas.
- **LACK OF AMBITION:-** Mental and physical laziness, lack of self-assertion (confidence), slowness in reaching decisions, easily influenced by others, the habit of criticizing others behind their backs, and flattering them to their faces, the habit of accepting defeat without protest, quitting an undertaking when opposed by others, suspicious of other people without cause, lacking in tactfulness of manner and speech, unwillingness to accept the blame for mistakes.

SYMPTOMS OF THE FEAR OF ILL HEALTH

- **AUTO-SUGGESTION:-** The habit of negative use of self-suggestion by looking for and expecting to find the symptoms of all kinds of disease. "Enjoying" imaginary illness, and speaking of it as being real. Talking to others of operations, accidents and other forms of illness.
- **HYPOCHONDRIA:-** The habit of talking of illness, concentrating upon disease, and expecting its appearance.
- **EXERCISE:-** Fear of ill health often interferes with proper physical exercise, and results in over-weight, by causing you to avoid outdoor life.
- **SUSCEPTIBILITY:-** Fear of ill health breaks down your natural body resistance, and creates a favorable condition for any form of disease you may contact.
- **SELF-CODDLING:-** The habit of making a bid for sympathy, using imaginary illness as the lure. (People often resort to this trick to avoid work). The habit of pretending to be ill to cover plain laziness, or to serve as an alibi for lack of ambition.
- **INTEMPERANCE:-** The habit of reading about illness, and worrying over the possibility of being stricken by it. The habit of reading patent medicine advertisements.

SYMPTOMS OF THE FEAR OF LOSS OF LOVE

- **JEALOUSY:-** The habit of being suspicious of friends and loved ones without any reasonable evidence of sufficient grounds, (jealousy is a form of dementia praecox which sometimes becomes violent without the slightest cause) The habit of accusing wife or husband of infidelity without grounds, general suspicions of everyone, absolute faith in no one.
- **FAULT FINDING:-** The habit of finding fault with friends, relatives, business associates and loved ones upon the slightest provocation, or without any cause whatsoever.
- **GAMBLING:-** The habit of gambling, stealing, cheating, and otherwise taking hazardous chances to provide money for loved ones, with the belief that love can be bought. The habit of spending beyond your means, with the object of making a favorable showing. Insomnia, nervousness, lack of persistence, weakness of will, lack of self-control, lack of self-reliance, bad temper.

SYMPTOMS OF THE FEAR OF OLD AGE

- **THE COMMONEST SYMPTOMS OF THIS FEAR ARE:-** The tendency to slow down and develop an inferiority complex at the age of mental maturity which is usually around age forty. Falsely believing yourself to be "slipping" because of age. (The truth is that our most useful years, mentally and spiritually, are those between forty and sixty) The habit of speaking apologetically of yourself as "being old" merely because you have reached the age of forty or fifty, instead, of reversing the rule and expressing gratitude for having reached the age of wisdom and understanding. The habit of killing off initiatives, imagination, and self-reliance by falsely believing yourself being too old to exercise these qualities. The habit of the man or woman of forty dressing with the aim of trying to appear much younger, and affecting mannerisms of youth; thereby, inspiring ridicule by both friends and strangers.

SYMPTOMS OF THE FEAR OF DEATH

- **THE GENERAL SYMPTOMS OF THIS FEAR ARE:-** The habit of thinking about dying, instead of making the most of LIFE, generally due to lack of purpose or lack of suitable occupation. The greatest of all remedies for the fear of death is a burning desire for achievement, backed by useful service to others.
- **THE COMMONEST SYMPTOMS OF THIS FEAR ARE:-** Ill-health, poverty, lack of appropriate occupation, disappointment over love, mental health problems, religious fanaticism.

OLD MAN WORRY

Worry is a state of mind based upon fear. Worry is caused by indecision, and indecision makes for an unsettled mind and an unsettled mind is helpless.

The six basic fears that I mentioned before translate to worry, and the antidote for fear and worry is the habit of making prompt and firm decision.

The exercise below will help you align yourself with the universe, and build self-confidence in your life choices.

A word of caution; this exercise might appear to be simple, but extra caution must be taken when contacting the universe. For this reason, this is why I suggested to you to first master the previous steps before attempting to put into practice the exercises I am going to be showing you now.

Concentration technique to align to the Universe

Start by closing your eyes and taking deep slow breaths, hold your breath in for a count of 7 and slowly breathing out in a count of 7, repeat this seven times. Once you begin to feel relaxed, bring your awareness to the room you are in, start expanding your energy field to merge with everything in the room, keep expanding your energy field to merge with your city, country, continent, the planet, and the galaxy, the whole universe.

Stay in this feeling for as long as necessary, then slowing start to bring back your awareness to the room you are in, and back to your body.

The purpose of this technique is to help you make firm and prompt decision on whatever life throws at you.

How to get rid of all the six basic fears

To relieve yourself forever of the fear of death, it's done by reaching a decision to accept death as an inescapable event of your life.

To wipe out the fear of poverty, you should reach a decision to get along with whatever wealth you can accumulate without worry.

You must put your foot down upon the neck of the fear of Criticism, by reaching a decision not to worry about what other people think, do, or say.

You must eliminate the fear of old age by reaching a decision to accept it, not as an handicap, but as a great blessing which carries with it wisdom, self-control and understanding not known to youth.

You must be sharp with thoughts of fear of ill-health by deciding to forget symptoms.

You should master the fear of loss of love by reaching a decision to get along without love, if that is necessary.

You should kill the habit of worry and all its forms by reaching a general blanket decision that nothing which life has to offer is worth the price of worry.

In *Thoughts of Success* and in our *Success Network Society,* we believe that we are here to be successful and we dedicate our lives in achieving success.

In *Thoughts Of Success,* we know that in order to truly be successful, you need to first find peace of mind by satisfying first your most immediate needs, e.g. Food and shelter, then everything else follows after.

**Everything in the universe begins in form of thought impulses; you have the power to feed your mind with whatever thought impulses you choose. You can certainly control your thoughts, influence it, and direct it to make your life what you want of it.

This awareness comes with great responsibility; use this knowledge constructively.

YOU ARE THE MASTER OF YOUR DESTINY.

HOW TO PROTECT YOURSELF AGAINST NEGATIVE INFLUENCES

In addition to the six basic fears, there is another fear which I refer to as the devil. And this devil is the negative influence we all suffer from; we are all affected by the devil of negative influence of other people and environment.

People who have accumulated great wealth always protect themselves against the devil of negative people and places! And if you so choose to be successful in any calling, you must train your mind to resist the devil of negative people and places.

You are now going to examine yourself very carefully to determine whether you are susceptible to negative influences.

Before you start yourself analysis, I would like to share with you an exercise which will help you protect yourself against negative influences.

To protect yourself against negative influences, whether of your own making or of the activities of negative people around you, you need to recognize that you have will power which you must put in constant use. You should also know, as a fact, that you and all other human beings are by nature, lazy, indifferent and suggestible to all suggestions which harmonize with your weakness.

You should recognize that you are by nature, suggestible to all of the six basic fears, and you should set up habits to counteract all of these fears.

You should also recognize that negative influences work on you through your subconscious mind, unnoticed, which makes them even more difficult to detect.

You must keep your mind closed against all people who depress or discourage you in any way.

You should deliberately seek the company of people who influence you to think and act for yourself.

Without a doubt, the most common weakness of all human beings is the habit of leaving their minds open to negative influences of other people.

This weakness is all the more damaging because most people do not recognize that they are cursed by it, and many who acknowledge it, neglect or refuse to correct this devil of negative influence until it becomes an uncontrollable part of their daily habits.

For those of you who are now choosing to experiment with the REAL self, a list has been prepared for you to self-analyze, so that you can reveal your true self or view yourself how others view you.

This manual maps out a complete path to success, YOU yourself have to be willing to decide to take control of your destiny forever, by putting in the right actions and necessary steps.

The following exercise is to be completed in your notebook, in the privacy of your own home.

It's best to carry out this exercise by asking yourself the following questions out loud, and answer them out loud to yourself. Answer the questions truthfully, and write down your answers in your notebook.

Some of these questions will be challenging and emotional, and it's very important, or should I say, it would be very beneficial for you if you can carry out this exercise once a year for the next 5 years.

SELF-ANALYSIS TEST QUESTIONS

1. DO YOU COMPLAIN OFTEN OF "FEELING BAD" AND IF SO, WHAT IS THE CAUSE?
2. DO YOU FIND FAULT WITH OTHER PEOPLE AT THE SLIGHTEST PROVOCATION?
3. DO YOU FREQUENTLY MAKE MISTAKES IN YOUR WORK, AND IF SO, WHY?
4. ARE YOU SARCASTIC AND OFFENSIVE IN YOUR CONVERSATION?
5. DO YOU DELIBERATELY AVOID THE ASSOCIATION OF ANYONE AND IF SO, WHY?
6. DO YOU SUFFER FREQUENTLY WITH INDIGESTION? IF SO, WHAT IS THE CAUSE?
7. DOES LIFE SEEM FUTILE AND THE FUTURE HOPELESS TO YOU? IF SO, WHY?
8. DO YOU LIKE YOUR OCCUPATION?
9. DO YOU OFTEN FEEL SELF-PITY, AND IF SO, WHY?
10. ARE YOU ENVIOUS OF THOSE WHO EXCEL MORE THAN YOU?
11. TO WHICH DO YOU DEVOTE MOST TIME, THINKING OF SUCCESS, OR OF FAILURE?
12. ARE YOU GAINING OR LOSING SELF-CONFIDENCE AS YOU GROW OLDER?
13. DO YOU LEARN SOMETHING OF VALUE FROM ALL MISTAKES?
14. ARE YOU PERMITTING SOME RELATIVES OR ANYONE TO WORRY YOU, IF SO, WHY?
15. ARE YOU SOMETIMES "IN THE CLOUDS" AND AT OTHER TIME, IN THE DEPTHS OF DESPONDENCY (low spirits)?
16. WHO HAS THE MOST INSPIRING INFLUENCE UPON YOU? WHAT IS THE CAUSE?
17. DO YOU TOLERATE NEGATIVE OR DISCOURAGING INFLUENCES WHICH YOU CAN AVOID?
18. ARE YOU CARELESS OF YOUR PERSONAL APPEARANCE? IF SO, WHEN AND WHY?
19. HAVE YOU LEARNED HOW TO "DROWN YOUR TROUBLES" BY BEING TOO BUSY TO BE ANNOYED BY THEM?

20. WOULD YOU CALL YOURSELF A "SPINELESS WEAKLING" IF YOU PERMITTED OTHERS TO DO YOUR THINKING FOR YOU?
21. DO YOU NEGLECT INTERNAL BATHING UNTIL AUTO-INTOXICATION MAKES YOU ILL-TEMPERED AND IRRITABLE?
22. HOW MANY PREVENTABLE DISTURBANCES ANNOY YOU, AND WHY DO YOU TOLERATE THEM?
23. DO YOU RESORT TO LIQUOR, NARCOTICS OR CIGARETTES TO "QUIET YOUR NERVES"? IF SO, WHY DON'T YOU TRY WILL POWER INSTEAD?
24. DOES ANYONE "NAG" YOU AND IF SO, FOR WHAT REASON?
25. DO YOU HAVE A DEFINITE MAJOR PURPOSE AND IF SO, WHAT IS IT AND WHAT PLAN HAVE YOU FOR ACHIEVING IT?
26. DO YOU SUFFER FROM ANY OF THE SIX BASIC FEARS? IF SO, WHICH ONE?
27. HAVE YOU A METHOD BY WHICH YOU CAN SHIELD YOURSELF AGAINST THE NEGATIVE INFLUENCES OF OTHERS?
28. DO YOU MAKE DELIBERATE USE OF AUTO-SUGGESTION TO MAKE YOUR MIND POSITIVE?
29. WHICH DO YOU VALUE THE MOST, YOUR MATERIAL POSSESSIONS OR YOUR PRIVILEGE OF CONTROLLING YOUR THOUGHTS?
30. ARE YOU EASILY INFLUENCED BY OTHERS, AGAINST YOUR OWN JUDGMENT?
31. HAS TODAY ADDED ANYTHING OF VALUE TO YOUR STOCK OF KNOWLEDGE OR STATE OF MIND?
32. DO YOU FACE SQUARELY THE CIRCUMSTANCES WHICH MAKE YOU UNHAPPY OR DO YOU SIDESTEP THE RESPONSIBILITY?
33. DO YOU ANALYZE ALL MISTAKES AND FAILURES AND TRY TO PROFIT BY THEM, OR DO YOU TAKE THE ATTITUDE THAT THIS IS NOT YOUR DUTY?
34. CAN YOU NAME THREE OF YOUR MOST DAMAGING WEAKNESSES? WHAT ARE YOU DOING TO CONTROL THEM?
35. DO YOU ENCOURAGE OTHER PEOPLE TO BRING THEIR WORRIES TO YOU FOR SYMPATHY?
36. DO YOU CHOOSE, FROM YOUR DAILY EXPERIENCES, LESSONS OR INFLUENCES WHICH AID IN YOUR PERSONAL ADVANCEMENT?
37. WHAT HABITS OF OTHER PEOPLE ANNOY YOU THE MOST?
38. DO YOU FORM YOUR OWN OPINIONS OR PERMIT YOURSELF TO BE INFLUENCED BY OTHER PEOPLE?
39. HAVE YOU LEARNED HOW TO CREATE A MENTAL STATE OF MIND WITH WHICH YOU CAN SHIELD YOURSELF AGAINST ALL DISCOURAGING INFLUENCES?
40. DOES YOUR OCCUPATION INSPIRE YOU WITH FAITH AND HOPE?
41. ARE YOU CONSCIOUS OF POSSESSING SPIRITUAL FORCES OF SUFFICIENT POWER TO ENABLE YOU TO KEEP YOUR MIND FREE FROM ALL FORCES OF FEAR?
42. DOES YOUR RELIGION HELP YOU KEEP YOUR OWN MIND POSITIVE?
43. DO YOU FEEL IT'S YOUR DUTY TO SHARE OTHER PEOPLE'S WORRIES?

44. IF YOU BELIEVE THAT "BIRDS OF A FEATHER FLOCK TOGETHER" WHAT HAVE YOU LEARNED ABOUT YOURSELF BY STUDYING THE FRIENDS WHOM YOU ATTRACT?
45. WHAT CONNECTION, IF ANY, DO YOU SEE BETWEEN THE PEOPLE WITH WHOM YOU ASSOCIATE MOST CLOSELY, AND ANY UNHAPPINESS YOU MAY EXPERIENCE?
46. COULD IT BE POSSIBLE THAT SOME PERSON WHOM YOU CONSIDER TO BE A FRIEND IS, IN REALITY, YOUR WORST ENEMY, BECAUSE OF THEIR NEGATIVE INFLUENCE ON YOUR MIND?
47. BY WHAT RULES DO YOU JUDGE WHO IS HELPFUL AND WHO IS DAMAGING TO YOU?
48. ARE YOUR INTIMATE ASSOCIATES MENTALLY SUPERIOR OR INFERIOR TO YOU?
49. HOW MUCH TIME OF EVERY 24 HOURS DO YOU DEVOTE TO;
    a) Your occupation
    b) Sleep
    c) Play and relaxation
    d) Acquiring useful knowledge
    e) Plain waste
50. WHO AMONG YOUR ACQUAINTANCES
    a) Encourages you most
    b) Cautions you most
    c) Discourages you most
    d) Helps you most
51. WHAT IS YOUR GREATEST WORRY? WHY DO YOU TOLERATE IT?
52. WHEN OTHERS OFFER YOU FREE, UNSOLICITED ADVICE, DO YOU ACCEPT IT WITHOUT QUESTION OR DO YOU ANALYSE THEIR MOTIVE?
53. WHAT ABOVE ALL ELSE, DO YOU MOST DESIRE? DO YOU INTEND TO ACQUIRE IT? ARE YOU WILLING TO SUBORDINATE ALL OTHER DESIRES FOR THIS ONE? HOW MUCH TIME DAILY DO YOU DEVOTE TO ACQUIRING IT?
54. DO YOU CHANGE YOUR MIND OFTEN? IF SO, WHY?
55. DO YOU USUALLY FINISH EVERYTHING YOU BEGIN?
56. ARE YOU EASILY INFLUENCED BY WHAT OTHER PEOPLE THINK OR SAY ABOUT YOU?
57. DO YOU CATER FOR PEOPLE BECAUSE OF THEIR SOCIAL OR FINANCIAL STATUS?
58. WHO DO YOU BELIEVE TO BE THE GREATEST PERSON LIVING? IN WHAT RESPECT IS THIS PERSON SUPERIOR TO YOU?
59. HOW MUCH TIME HAVE YOU DEVOTED TO STUDYING AND ANSWERING THESE QUESTIONS? (at least one day is necessary for the analysis and answering of the entire list)

If you have just finished answering these questions, no doubt you now know more about yourself, which previously didn't even acknowledge.

Don't be mad at yourself, remember you are a creature of habit and the most important thing to remember is YOU have absolute control over your thought, and your thoughts are the means by which you can control your destiny.

Mind control is the result of self-discipline and habit; you either control your mind, or it controls you. There is no halfway.

The most practical way of controlling your mind is being busy with a definite purpose, backed by a definite plan.

LAST NOTE
I would like to wrap up this manual with one burning question of mine; WHY do some people not succeed?
Here is a list of fifty-seven alibis people create in their mind, and which blocks them from attaining the success they are dying for:

If I didn't have a wife and family…..
If I had enough "pull"……
If I had money….
If I had a good education ….
If I could get a job ….
If I had good health …..
If I only had time ……..
If times were better ……
If other people understood me …..
If conditions around me were only different ……
If I could live my life over again ……
If I did not fear what they would say …..
If I had been given a chance ……
If I now had a chance ……
If other people didn't have it in for me ……
If nothing happens to stop me …….
If I were only younger …..
If I could only do what I want …..
If I had been born rich …….
If I could meet the right people ……
If I had the talent that some people have ……
If I had dared assert myself ……..
If I only had embraced past opportunities …….
If people didn't get on my nerves …..
If I didn't have to keep the house and look after the children …..
If I could save money …..
If the boss only appreciated me …..
If I only had somebody to help me ……
If my family understood me ……
If I lived in a big city …..

If I could just get started …..
If I were only free ……
If I had the personality of some people …….
If I were not so fat ……
If my talents were known ……..
If I could just get a break …..
If I could only get out of debt …..
If I hadn't failed ……
If I only knew how …..
If everybody didn't oppose me …..
If I didn't have so many worries …..
If I could marry the right person …..
If people weren't so dumb ……
If my family were not so extravagant …..
If I were sure of myself …..
If luck were not against me ……
If I had not been born under the wrong star …..
If it were not true that "what is to be will be"…….
If I did not have to work so hard …….
If I hadn't lost my money …..
If I lived in a different neighbourhood …..
If I didn't have a past …..
If I only had a business of my own ….
If others would only listen to me ….
If I only stayed ……
If only I did it till the end…..

WHAT SUCCESS CONSISTS OF

Definite chief aim
Habit of saving
Self-confidence
Imagination
Initiative
Leadership
Enthusiasm
Self-control
Doing more than paid for
Pleasing personality
Accurate thought
Concentration
Co-operation
Failure
Tolerance
Golden rule
The master mind

INDEX

This manual was inspired by Napoleon Hill's book, Think and Grow Rich, by Tom Butler-Bowdon http://www.butler-bowdon.com/think-and-grow-rich.html

Printed in Great Britain
by Amazon